My Bike

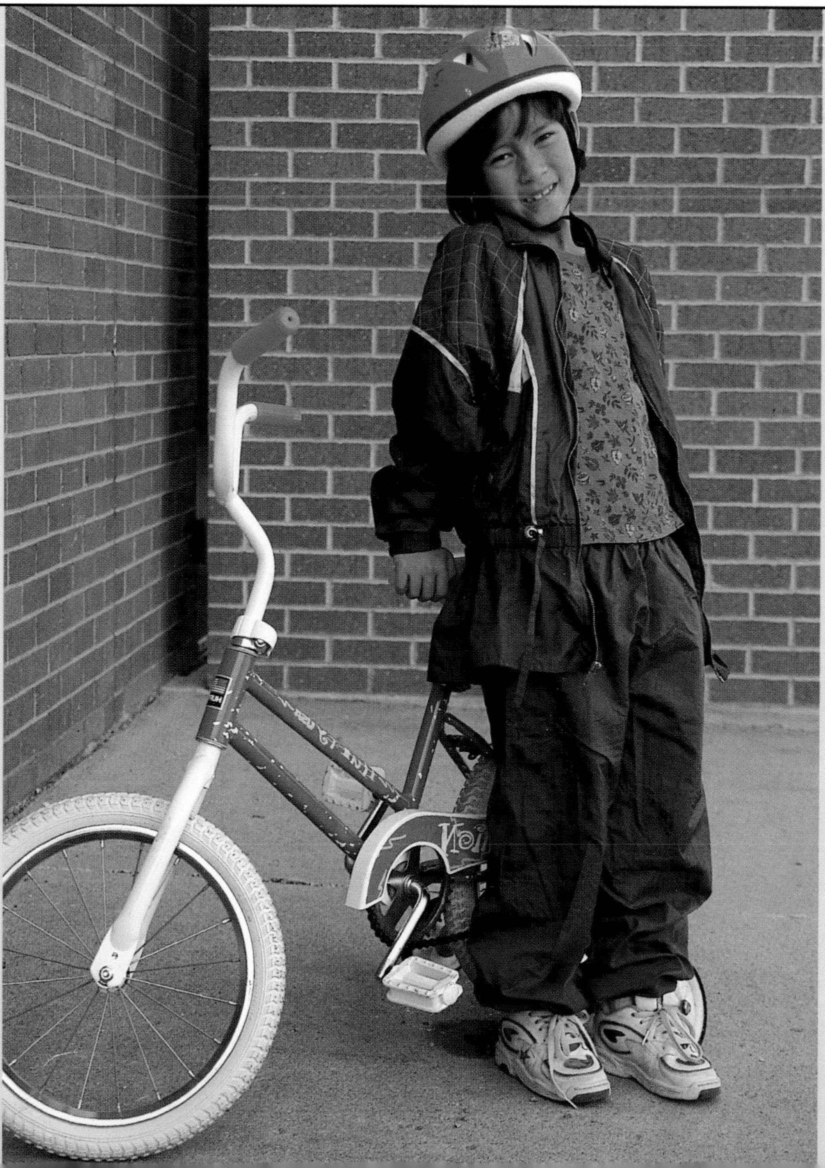

My bike has four wheels.

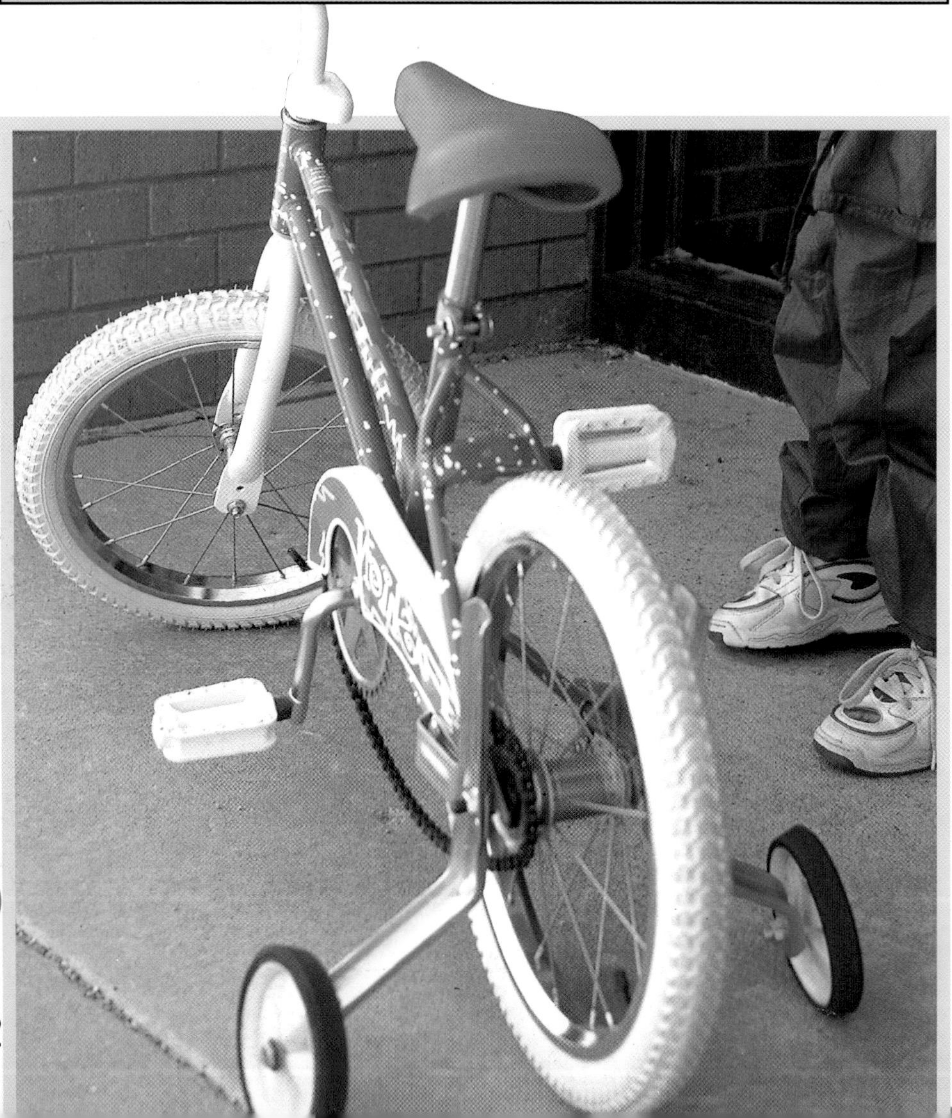

I can ride my bike.

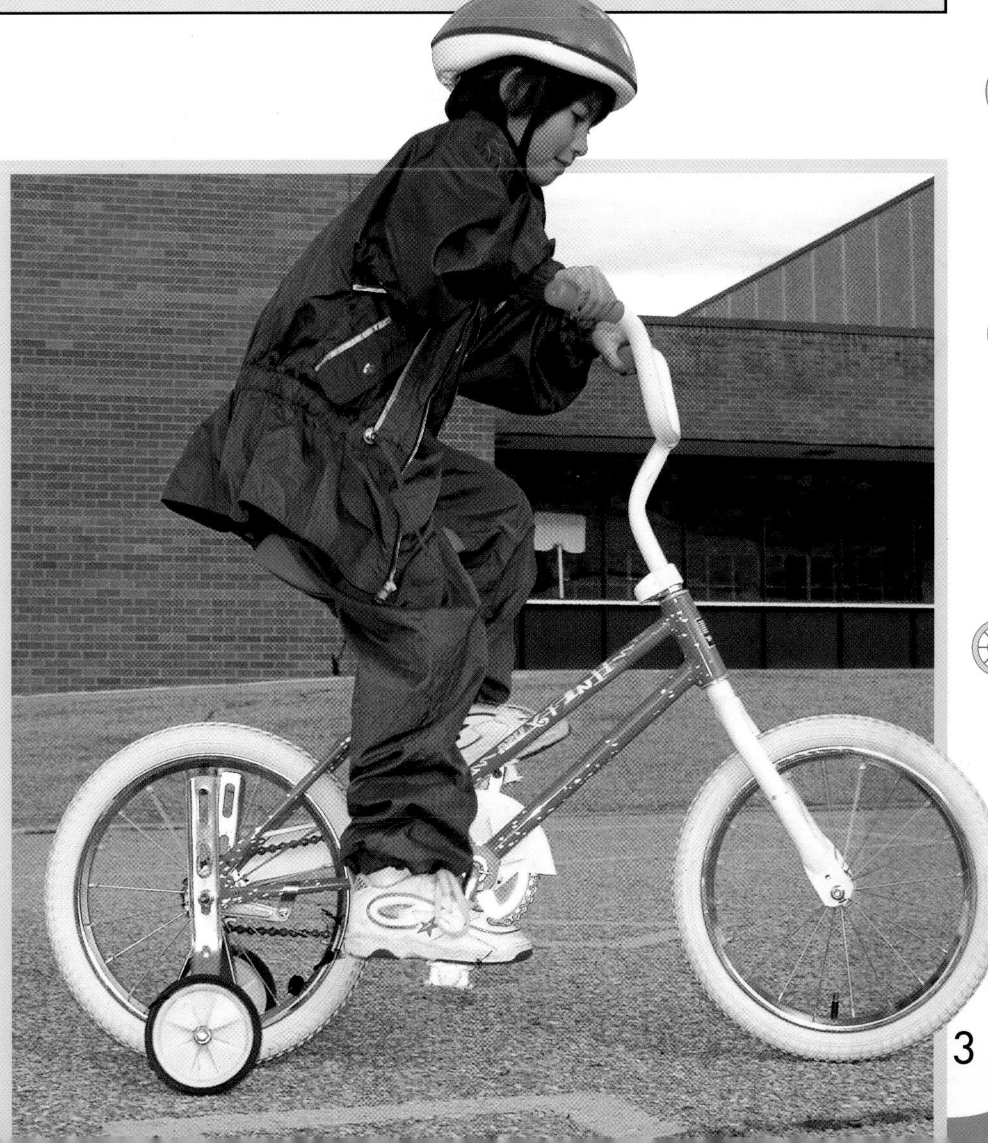

Now my bike
has two wheels.

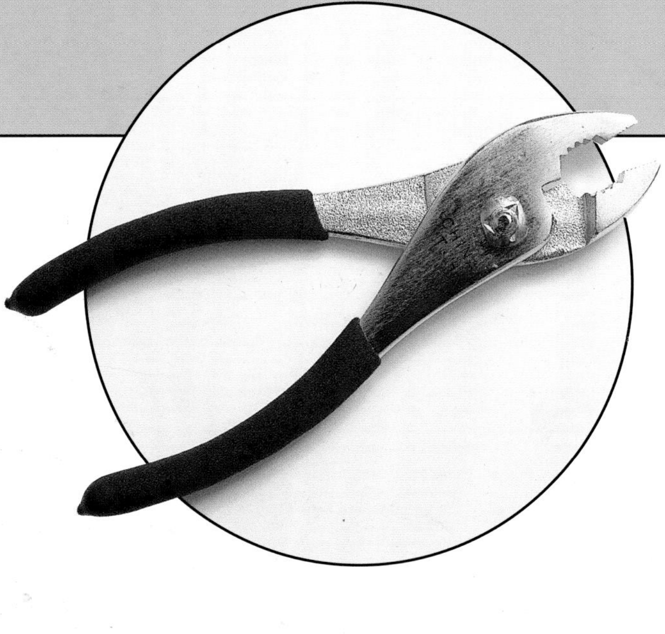

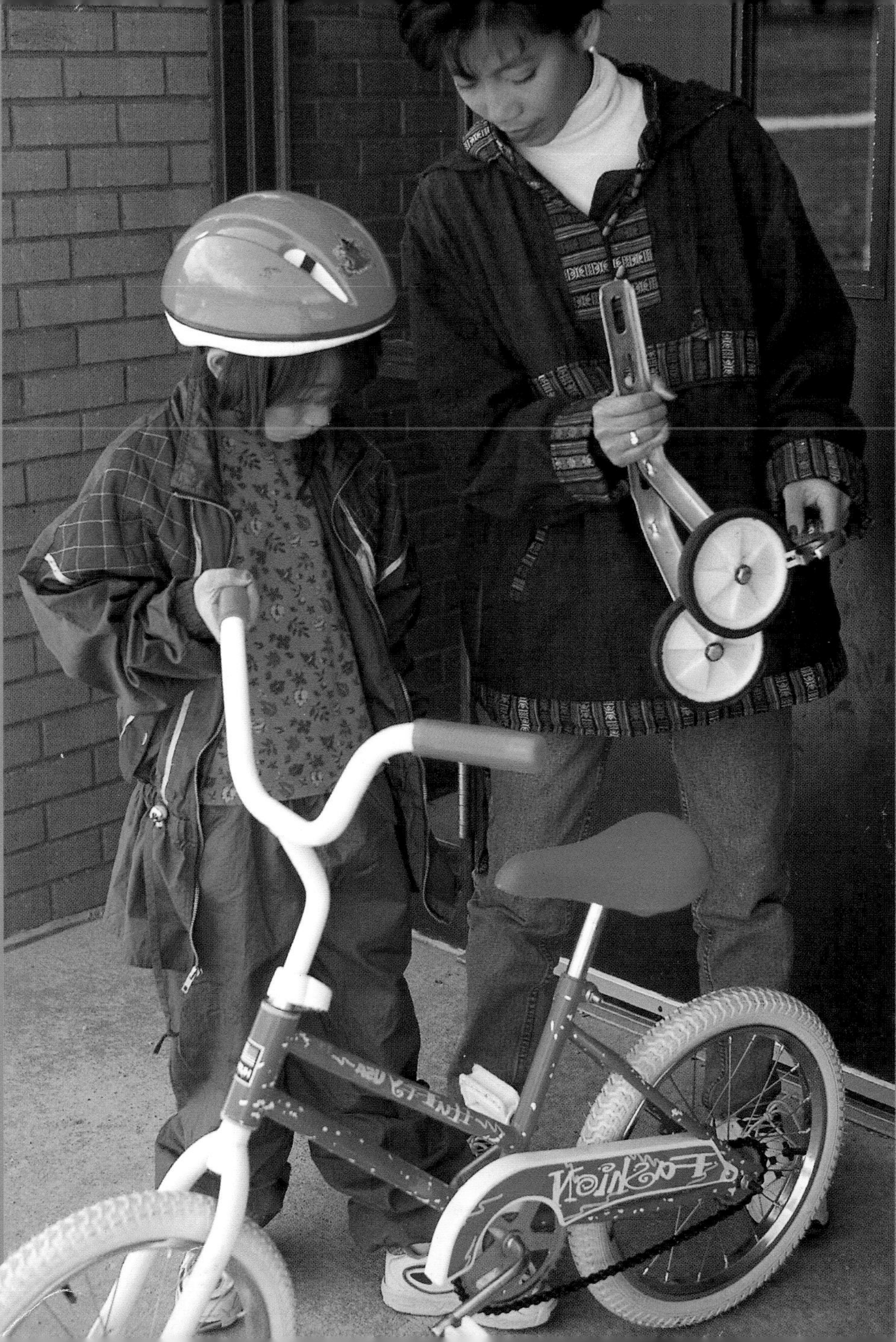

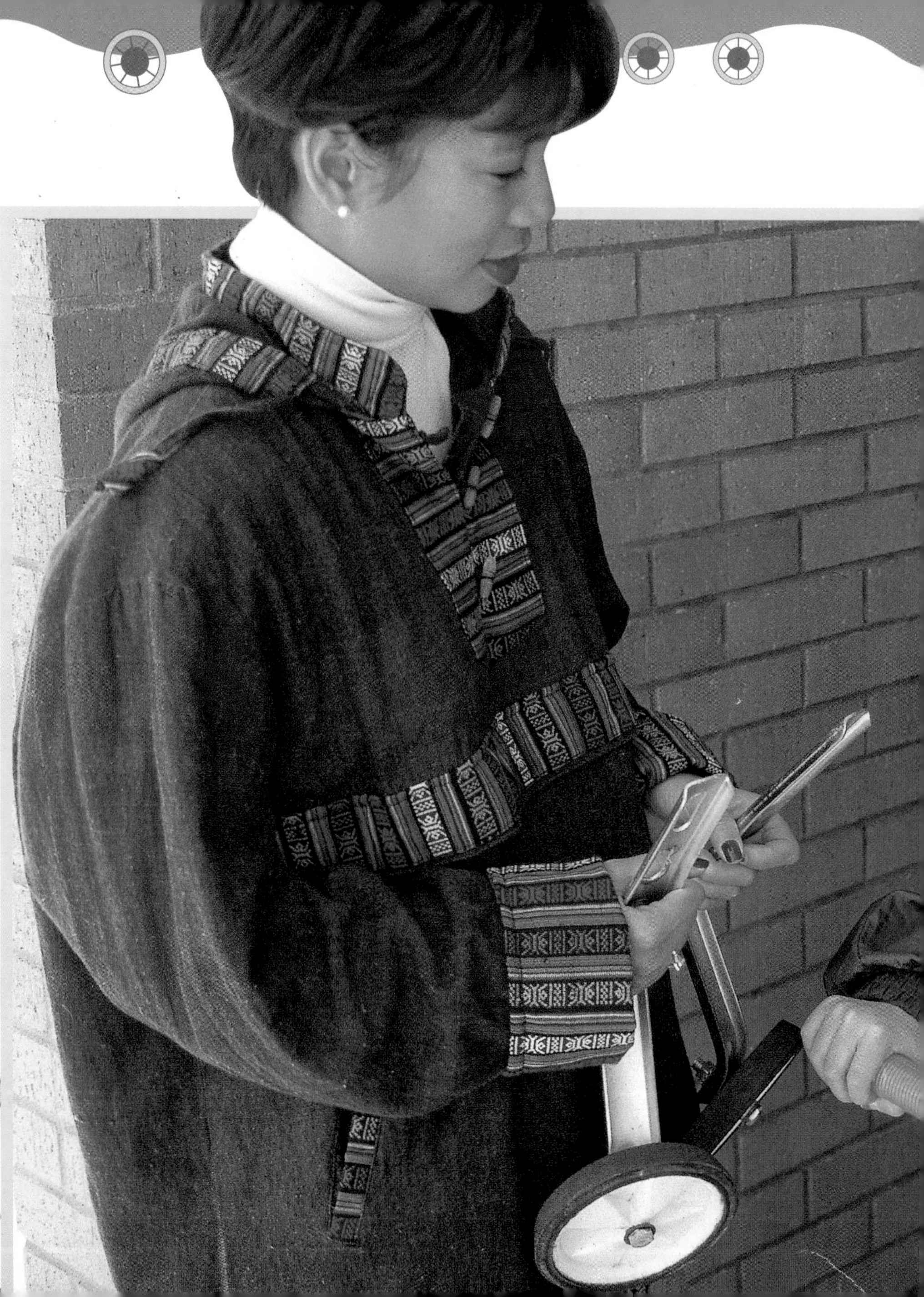

Can I ride my bike?

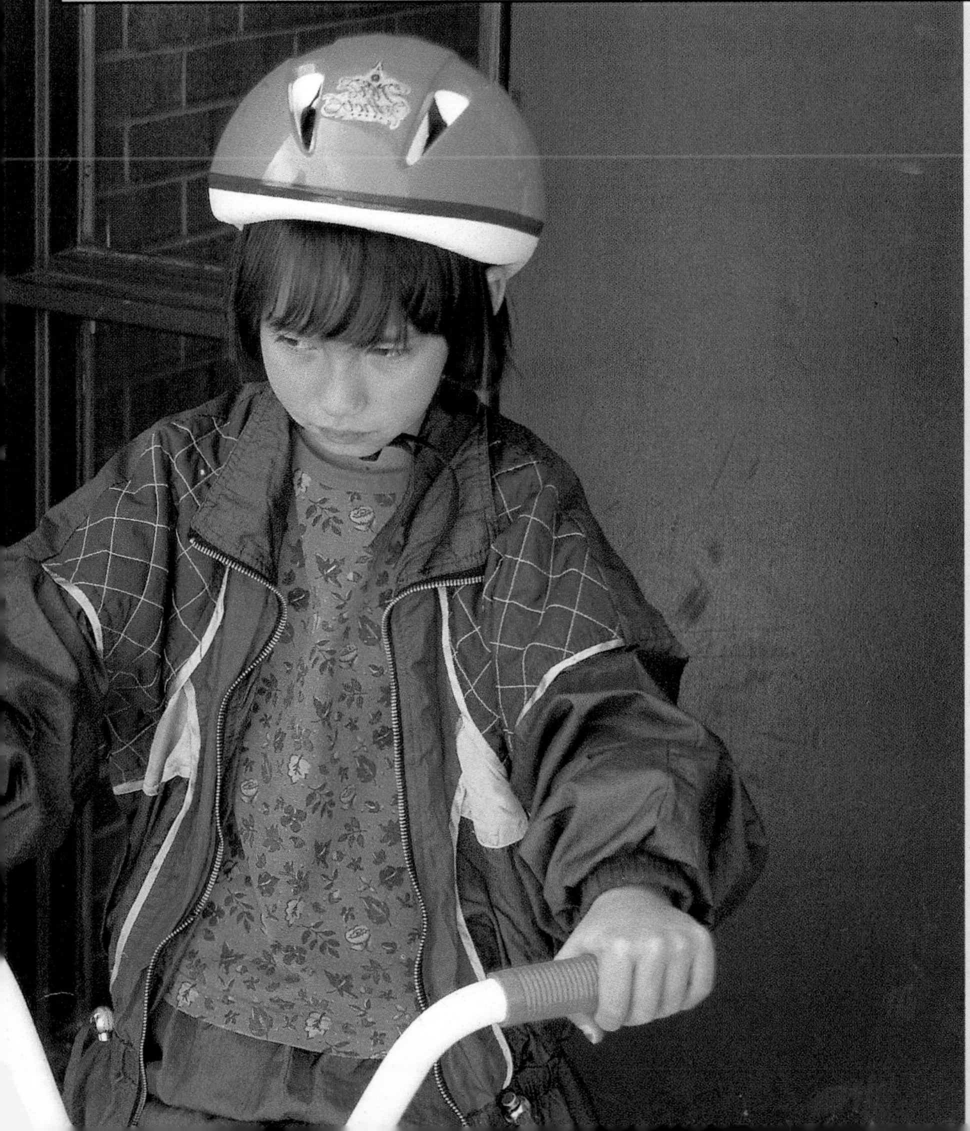

Mom holds me.

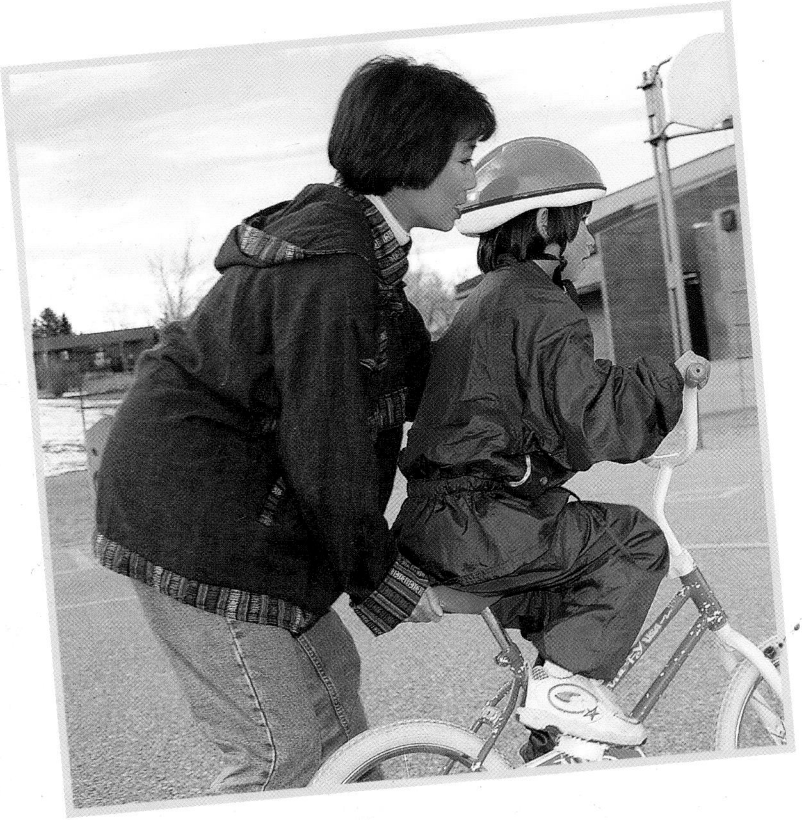

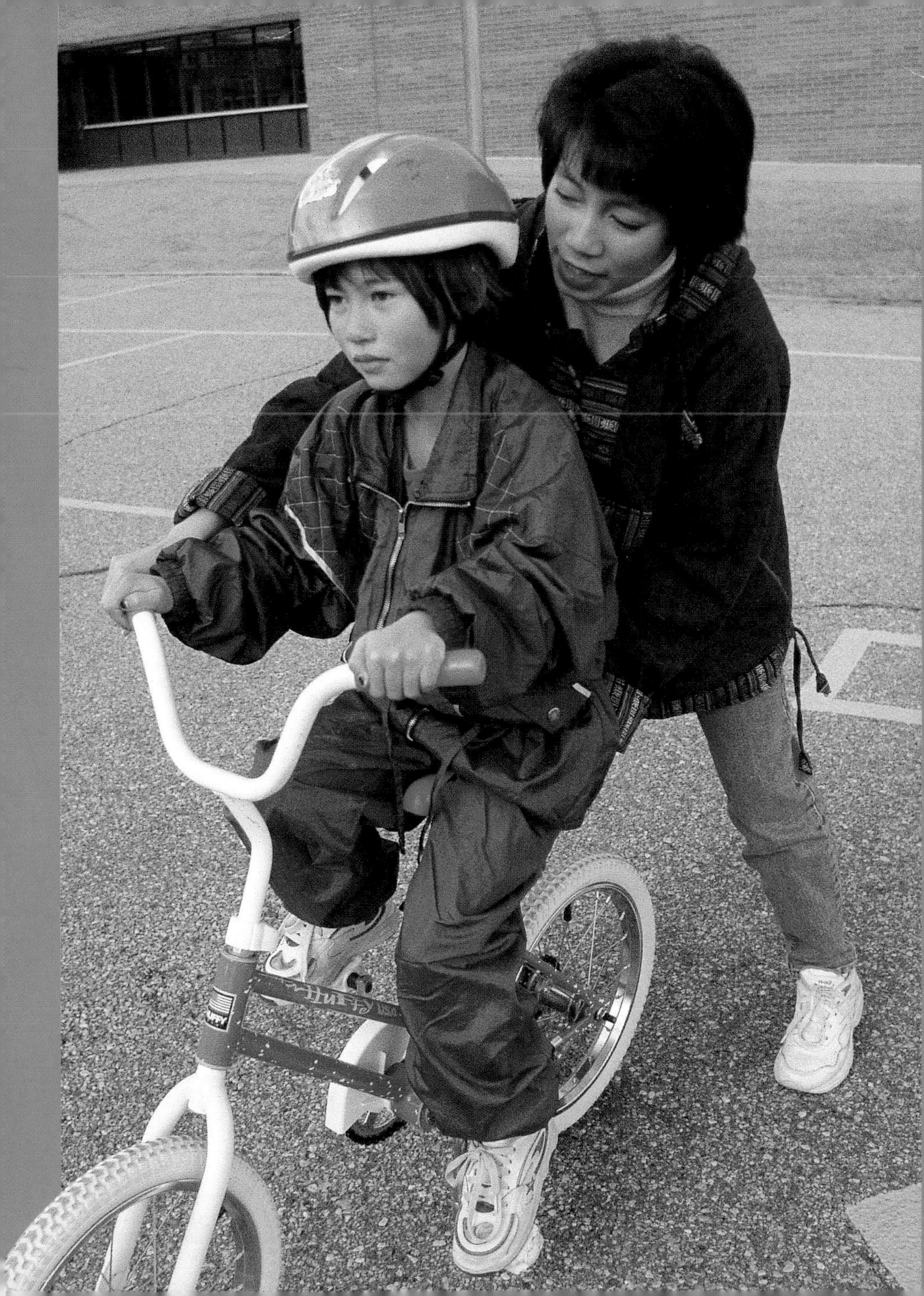

Mom lets go.

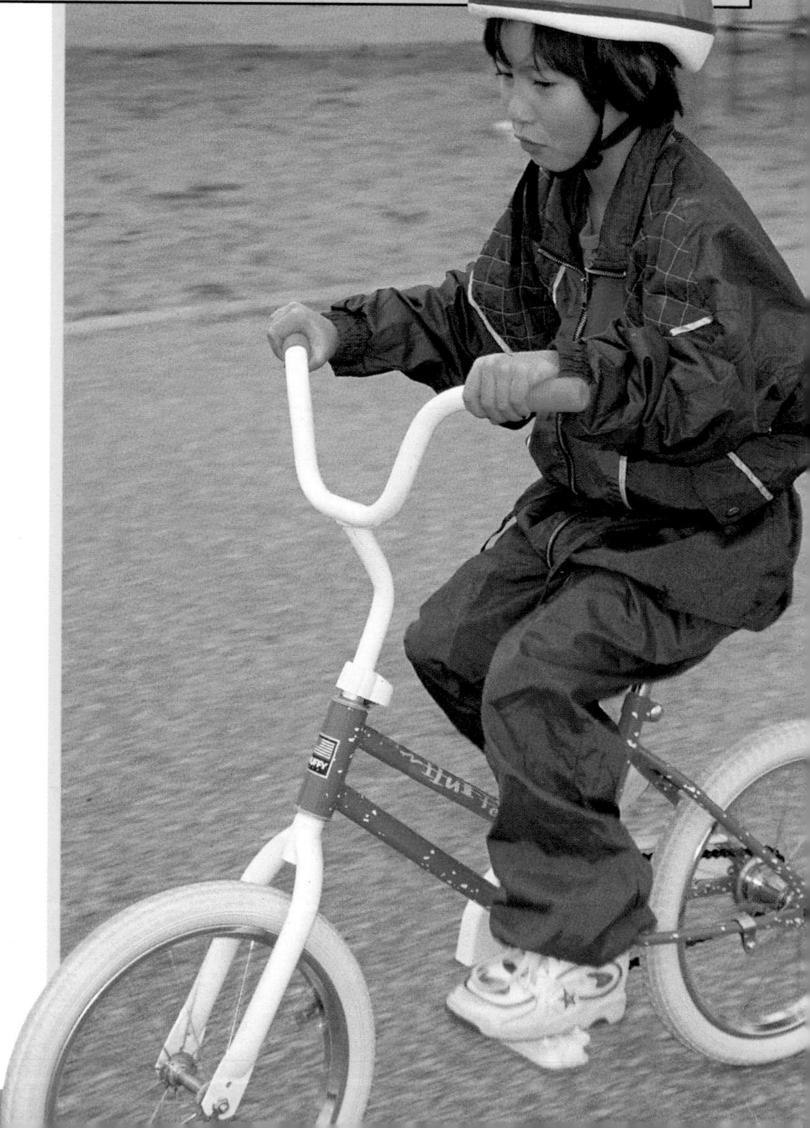

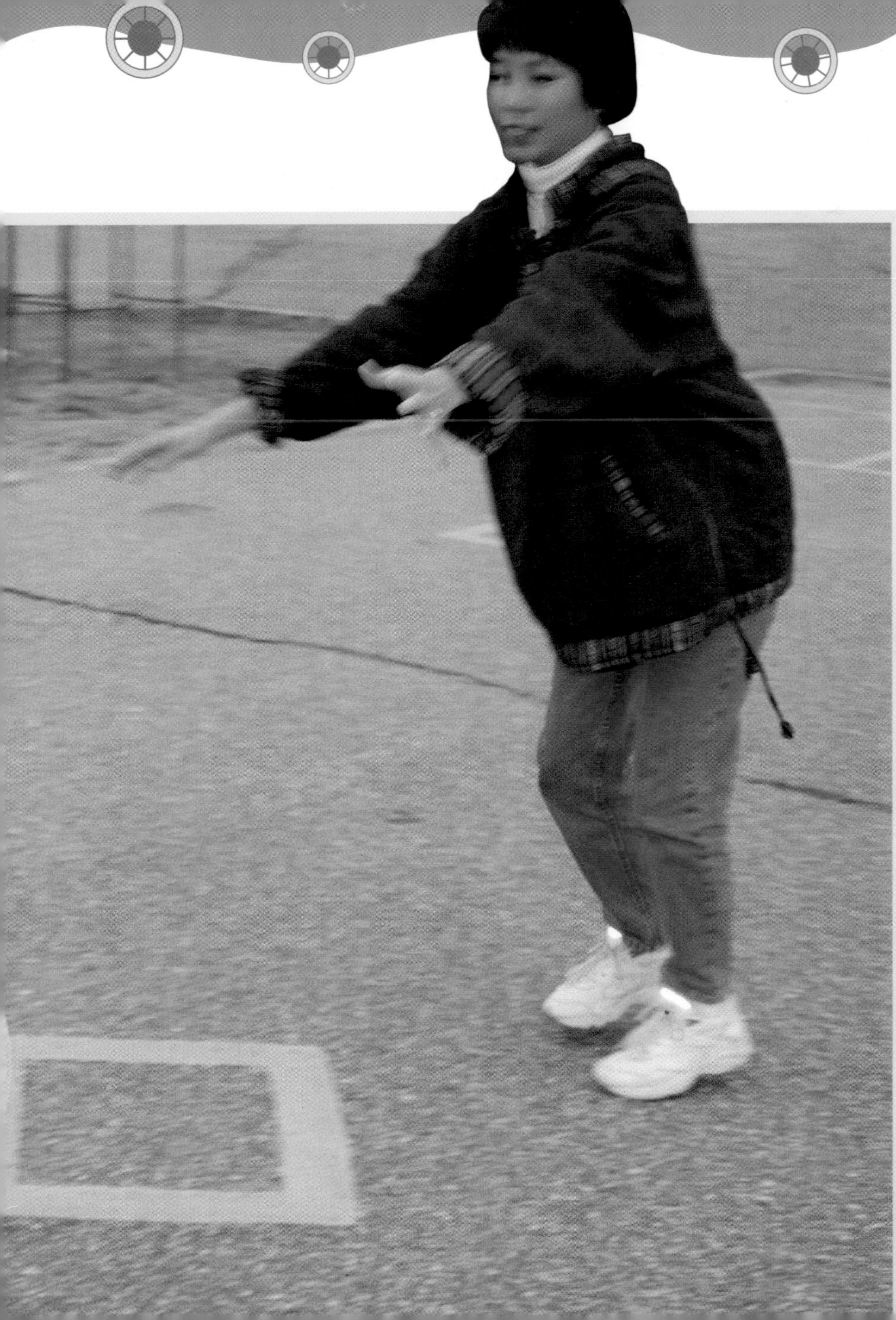

I fall down.

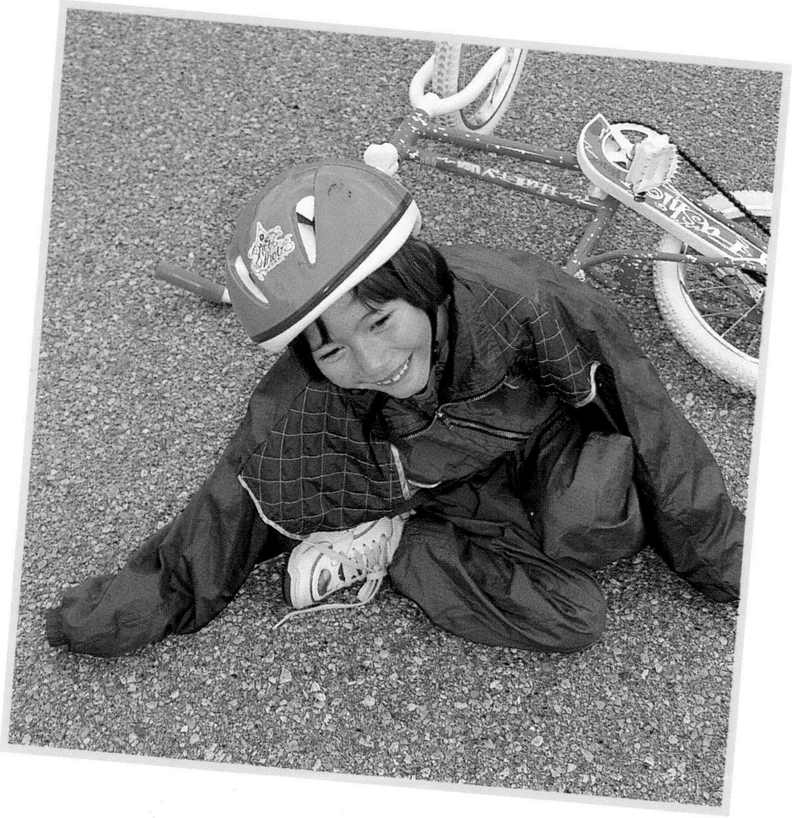

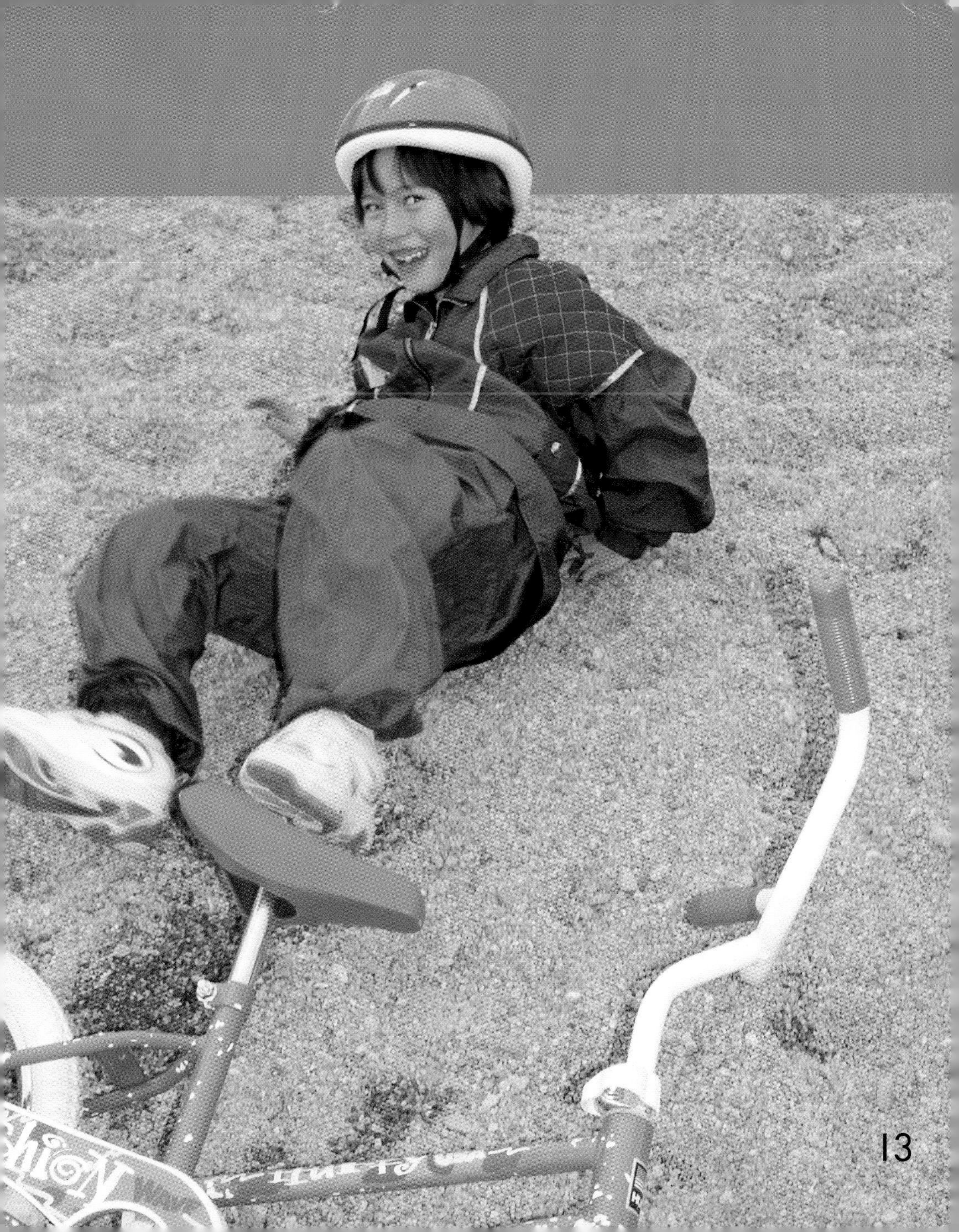

I get up.

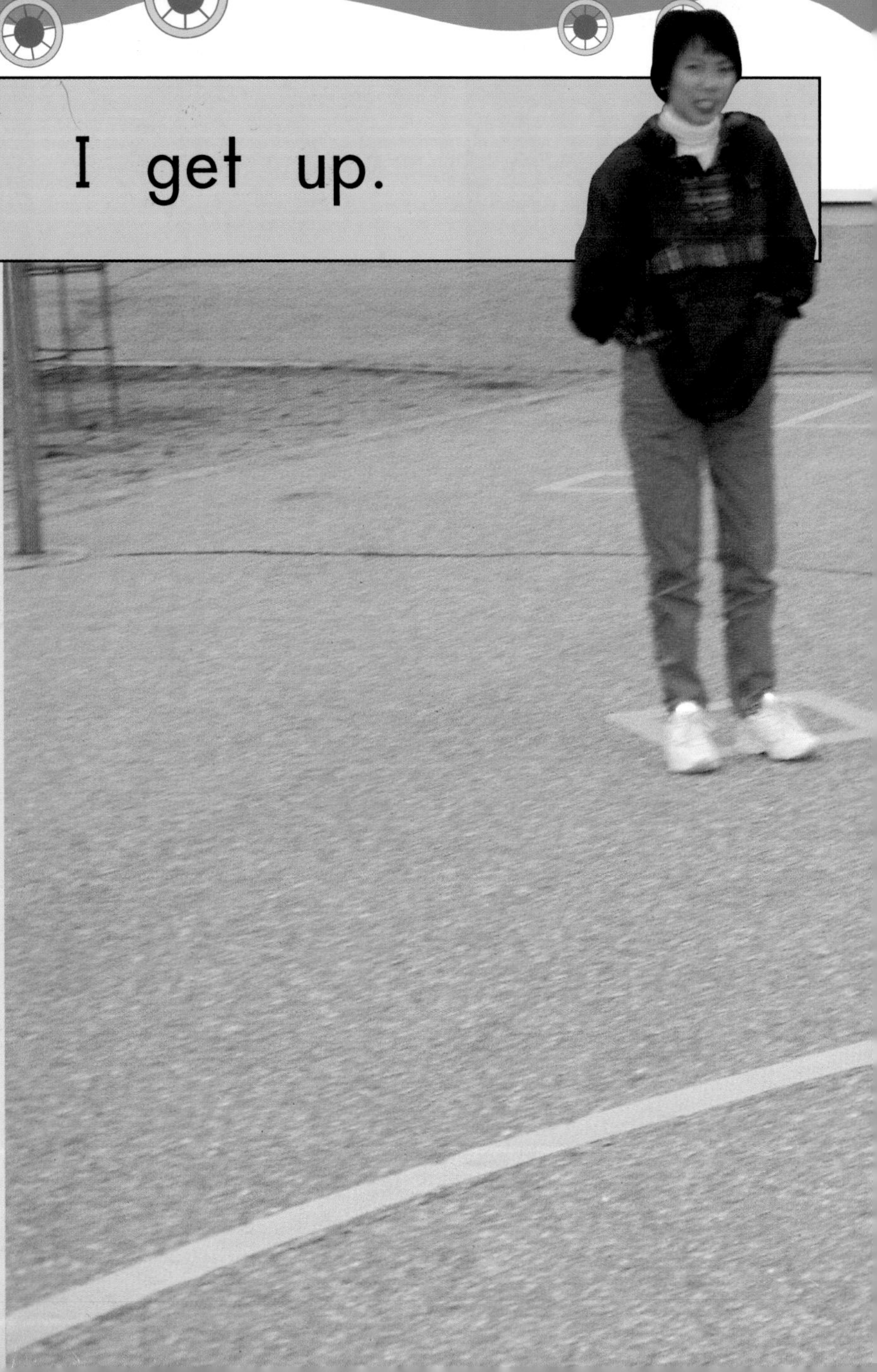

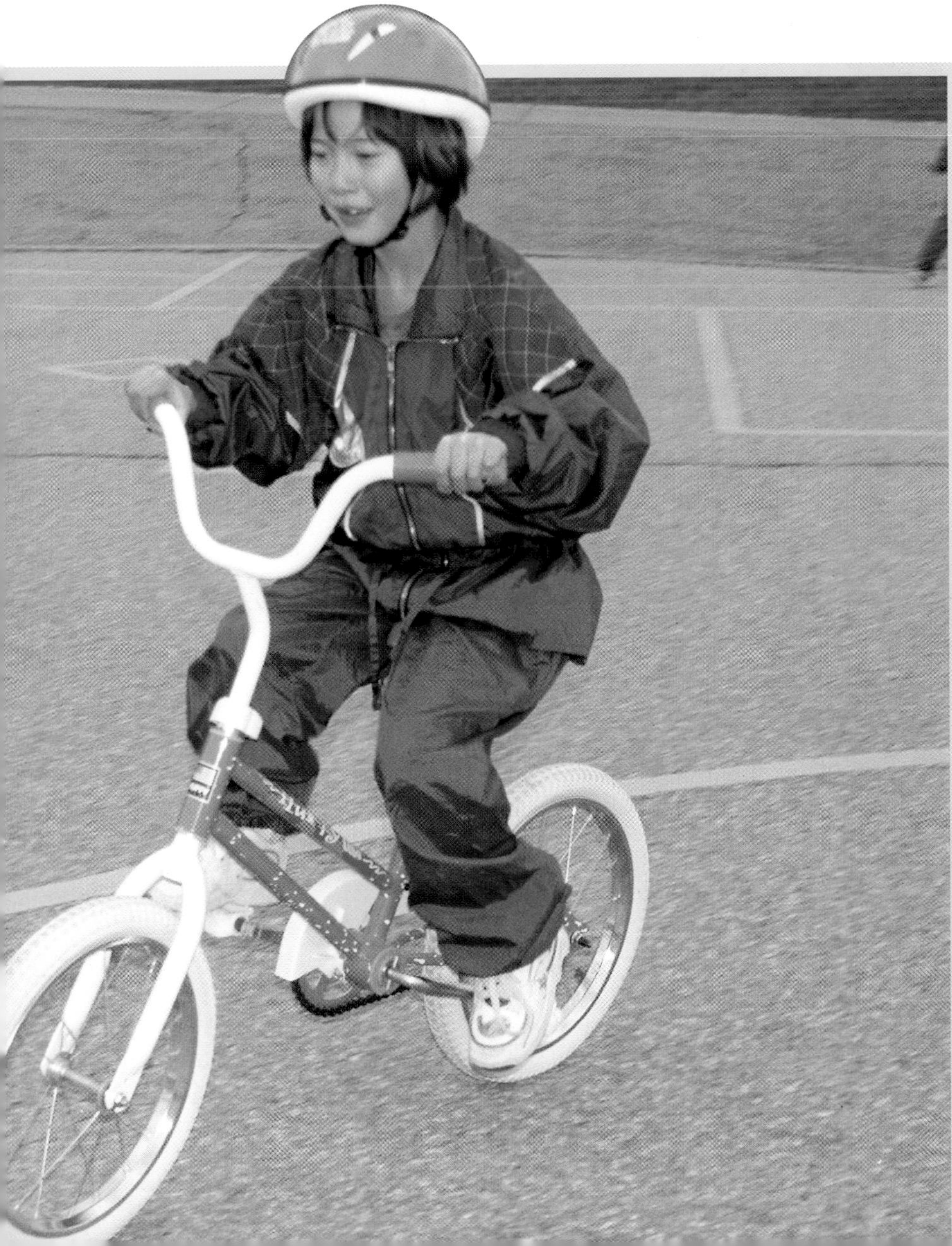

I can ride my bike!

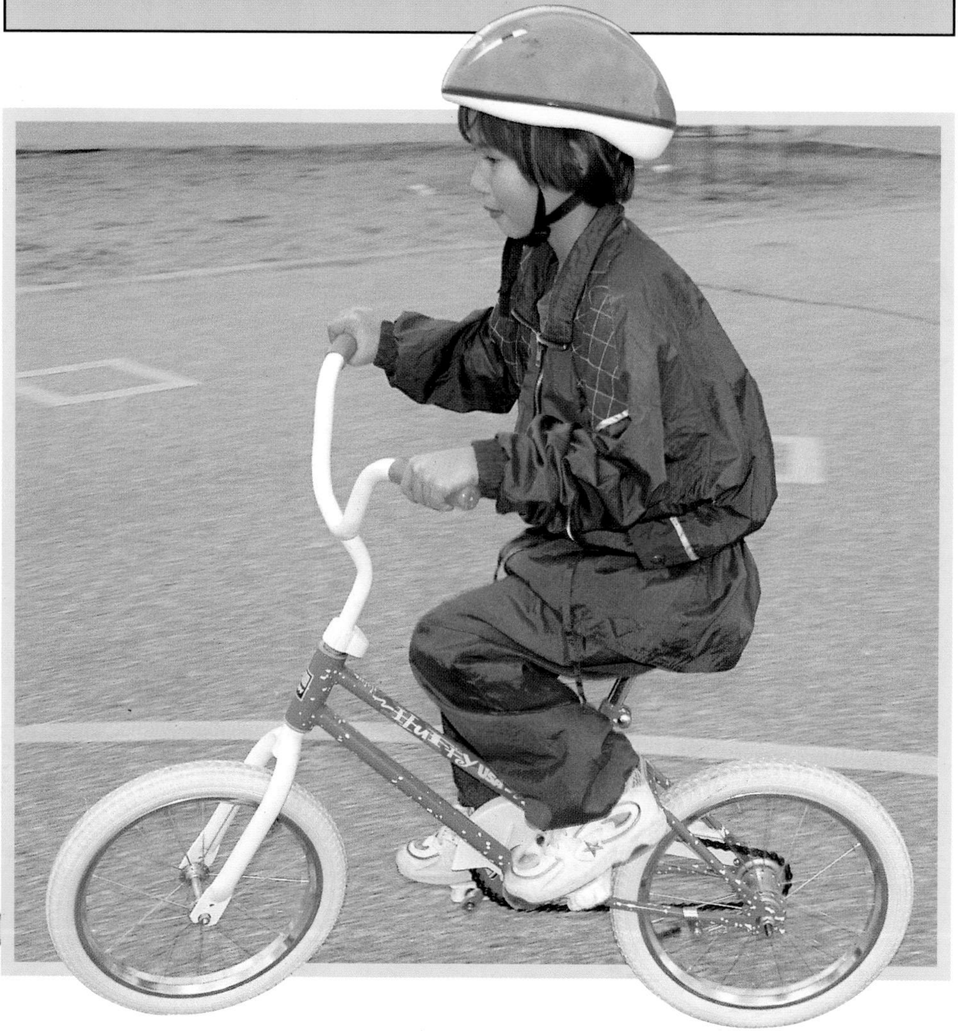